CALIFORNIA

A PICTURE BOOK TO REMEMBER HER BY

Designed by
DAVID GIBBON

Produced by
TED SMART

Photography by
EDMUND NAGELE

CRESCENT

INTRODUCTION

In their ruthless search for wealth, the Conquistadores of the 16th and 17th centuries were largely responsible for the discovery and settlement of Spain's colonies in the New World. Although it was discovered in 1542, California was not colonized until 1769, and only then because news had reached the Spanish government that explorers and fur traders from Czarist Russia were about to settle there.

Two expeditions were sent from Spain, one by land and the other by sea, to lay claim to this land. Of the three ships that set out only two reached their destination and many of those aboard suffered from scurvy. The overlanders, however, fared much better.

Amongst these early adventurers were missionaries – small groups of Jesuit and Franciscan fathers – under the leadership of Junipero Serra, eager to convert the tribes of Red Indians who dwelt in California. The Indians' existence was a meagre one and they hunted rodents and picked roots, fruit, acorns and wild rice. When the missionaries arrived they introduced new crops, taught crafts and offered baptism and education. Many of the Indians reacted strongly against this intrusion into their traditional way of life. Their numbers were greatly diminished as they fell victim to the white man's diseases such as chicken pox and measles – diseases against which they had little or no resistance. The fathers, however, persevered and eventually twenty-one Missions were built in the valleys between San Francisco and San Diego and Christianity started to spread.

Other Spanish settlers were granted huge tracts of land for cattle rearing, but their attempts at farming were not really successful and with their failure to discover the rich minerals California soon passed into the control of Mexico, in whose hands it remained for more than sixty years. In 1848 it was ceded to the U.S.A. and two years later became the 31st State of the Union. However, the influence of Spain and Mexico still remains to this day – especially in the place names and the architecture.

Prior to 1848, favourable reports of conditions in the West were passed down by Charles Fremond, an explorer, and writers like James Fennimore Cooper and Richard Henry Dana. Dana published a graphic description of the tallow and hide trade under the title 'Two Years before the Mast' – a book that undoubtedly stimulated immigration to California, for the East was starting to fill up and as virgin land was becoming scarce so prospects suddenly seemed much better in the West.

Pioneer farmers began to move across the Prairies and the Rockies with five or six months' supplies of food, ammunition, tools, spare parts for their wagons and extra animals. Obstacles were many, food and water were often in short supply, hostile Indians stole their horses and cattle and killed many of the inadequately protected families. In the early days many of the wagons had to be abandoned when the Rockies were reached and the pioneers continued on horseback. By 1845, however, trails to California and nearby Oregon were established, suitable for the heavy covered wagons. It is estimated that between 1845 and 1860, 170,000 people travelled overland from the Mississippi to California.

A very important event happened in 1848 that encouraged settlers, not just from the east, but from several countries around the world. This was the discovery of large quantities of gold in the Sacramento Valley, in the foothills of the Sierra Nevada. With this discovery the Gold Rush started in earnest. Towns sprang up almost overnight to accommodate the eager prospectors who arrived with pickaxes, shovels and, indeed, anything they could use to dig for the precious metal and thereby make their fortunes. And yet, ten years later, the days of the individual prospector were virtually finished; large companies had taken over the expensive but profitable task of extracting ore from the deep veins. As for the gold-diggers, some returned to their old lives but others, the gold-fever now in their blood, moved on, seeking their fortunes at new sites such as the Fraser River and the Klondyke in Canada. Mining still flourishes in California but oil now outstrips gold in importance.

The completion of the Transcontinental Railroad in 1869 brought many more settlers to the 'Sunshine State' with its favourable climate and fertile soils and even today California is the most populated and fastest-growing state in the U.S.A. It boasts some of the most beautiful and diverse scenery in the whole country – dramatic deserts, national parks with giant sequoia trees, sparkling lakes and waterfalls, sweet-smelling orange and lemon groves and extensive vineyards, as well as surf-washed beaches along 11,000 miles of Pacific coastline.

California's towns and cities include sprawling Los Angeles with its famous suburb of Hollywood, glamour capital of the world, whose studios still retain the atmosphere of film-making's affluent past. To the north is the unusual and lovely city of San Francisco, perched on a hill overlooking the spectacular Golden Gate Bridge. Cable-cars and elegant Victorian mansions, fine restaurants and fashionable shops belie the fact that the city's past is so closely linked with the Gold Rush or that in 1906 an earthquake and the resulting fires caused widespread devastation.

Another Gold Rush town is Sacramento, the State Capital and an important inland port and agricultural centre. Much farther south, near the Mexican border, is California's oldest town, San Diego, rich in Spanish-Mexican history. In contrast is Palm Springs, a rich man's playground on the edge of the Mojave Desert, renowned for its fine climate as well as some three dozen golf courses. The town is divided up into mile squares, every other one belonging to the Agua Caliente Indians, the original inhabitants of the land.

The very land has been affected by the large numbers of people who have chosen to make their homes in California. Concrete highways, skyscrapers of steel and glass, and smog lying in the ever-expanding towns and cities are a sad reminder of 20th century progress. However, the magnificent natural landscape still predominates and planning for the future includes the continued protection of the most outstanding beauty spots, together with more sympathetic designs for buildings and roads and curbs on pollution. It is essential that the 'Sunshine State' remains as unspoilt as possible in order to allow future generations the pleasure and enjoyment of living in such an outstanding part of the country.

The golden glow of sunset floods Pigeon Point Lighthouse *left*.

San Diego is California's southernmost city and offers a wealth of attractions to the discerning visitor. In the beautiful Balboa Park *above left and centre left* are these lovely examples of Spanish baroque architecture, whilst *below left* can be seen the low white building of the Natural History Museum. Picturesque Sherman Gilbert House *above* stands in the Old Town Historical State Park and was built in 1887, and *below,* Mission San Diego de Alcala was California's first mission founded by Juniper Serra on the 16th July 1769.

Coronado Island is a popular resort reached by a huge bridge whose stilt-like structure can be seen *below right.* Looking from the island the San Diego coastline is seen *above right* and *below far right* the incredibly wide highways leading downtown.

La Jolla, lapped by the blue Pacific *left, top right and centre right* has a magnificent coastline comparable to that of the French Riviera.
The historic gable roofed Hotel Del Coronado *below* is on an island of the same name, below which can be seen the Old Point Loma Lighthouse, Gabrillo National Monument, whilst "Hanse House" at Carlsbad by the Sea *bottom right,* is another lovely example of a bygone era.

San Diego Zoo in Balboa Park contains the world's largest collection of wild animals with over 4,500 species and some of its magnificent residents are pictured here including the proud peacock, African lions, Arctic polar bear, Indian elephants and flamingoes – all of which enjoy the spacious, largely unfenced area that is a delight to its many visitors.

Sea World in Mission Bay Park attracts scores of people *centre right* to the many and varied aquatic performances held each day. *Above and above right* "Shamu" the killer whale goes through his routine whilst *below right* the dolphins leap in concert to the delight of the crowd. Fountains play *below* in the lush environment that Sea World affords its guests.

One fifth of California's State is covered by arid desert which is divided into two National Monuments and one State Park, namely Anza-Borrego pictured on these pages. In this lonely region with its hot, shifting sand, the pools of colour created by the flowering cacti are a welcome relief. Some examples can be seen *below*, in the "Prickly Pear" beaver-tail cactus and *right* in Englemenn's Hedgehog Cactus, which are amongst the many flowering species to be found within the desert region.

Death Valley National Monument holds fourteen square miles of undulating sand dunes. The powerful waves *left* whose basic contours remain unaltered from year to year nevertheless change face according to the wind's velocity as it drives across the open plains. Zabriskie Point is seen *below,* from where can be viewed the huge carved craters of Funeral Mountains, and *right* looking like the Lunar surface is Devil's Golfcourse, with its crusty ridges consisting almost entirely of salt.

Two further views from Zabriskie Point *left and right* showing the sculptured mountains fashioned by nature's hand, and *below* looking like a vast sheet of cracked paving stone is the Bristol Dry Lake near Amboy in San Bernadino County.

Spring brings a splash of colour to the sombre background in Death Valley *centre left,* and *below left* is the incredible fort-like structure of "Scotty's Castle" set amidst the mountains. In Kern County lies Red Rock Canyon whose chiselled rock formation can be seen *below.*

The modern face of Los Angeles is reflected in its glossy buildings and wide highways: *above* the City Centre and Harbour Freeway, *centre left* the intersection at Century Plaza and *below left* Hollywood and Vine. Dwarfed by the Twin Towers rising in the background is the ABC Entertainment Centre in Century Plaza *above left*, whilst the graceful City Hall *right and below* stands serenely in the afternoon sunshine.

The many varied facets of Los Angeles are discernible in its widely differing styles of architecture. *Above* can be seen the ultra-modern Mark Taper Forum, one of three theatre complexes in the Music Centre, whilst *below,* in sharp contrast, is the graceful Huntington Library with its fine statues set in smooth green lawns. Fast flowing traffic moves easily along wide, palm fringed Western Avenue *above left* and in Westwood Village *below left;* whilst still more traffic races past the Wilshire Building *centre left.*

At Universal Studios, in glamorous
Hollywood, visitors can take a two hour
tram tour and delight in the make-
believe world of the movies *right*.

Preserved in concrete the hand and
footprints of the stars can be seen
below at Mann's, originally Grauman's,
Chinese Theatre.

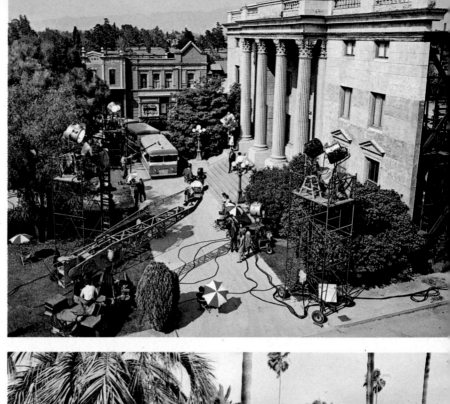

Beverley Hills is the home of many
movie stars and its lush, tropical
atmosphere is typified in the Plaza
centre right with its exotic palms and
colourful blooms.

Pasadena is most famous for its Rose
Bowl Stadium where, on New Year's
Day, football fans crowd the arena to
watch the classic championship match.
The ornate City Hall *right* clearly
reflects the Spanish inspired
architecture so prevalent in the 1920's.

Ports of Call Village-Whaler's Wharf, in San Pedro, is a unique tourist attraction reminiscent of the old fishing communities and villages of the early 19th century *this page*. In the northern area lies the Village, with its weather-board houses and cobbled streets lit by gas-lamps. To the south lies Whaler's Wharf with its Clipper ships and bluewater fishermen, and both areas offer excellent speciality restaurants and shops.

In the heart of Los Angeles lies the Pueblo, whose Mexican village atmosphere is most keenly felt in Olvera Street *this page.* Here in the sunshine stalls can be found laden with colourful merchandise and also cheerful street musicians who frequently take part in the many festivities held in the area.

Lying in a magnificent 200 acre estate in San Marino, is Huntington, famous for its Botanical Gardens *below,* Art Gallery and Library. Within the gardens is the superb "Cactus Garden", in which incredible giant cacti can be seen *left and above.*

Mary's Gate Village is sited at Long Beach *above right and below right* where lies berthed the famous Queen Mary *centre right,* whose conversion from the world's largest passenger liner includes a sea museum, shops, restaurants and a hotel.

The wonderful, magical world of Disneyland at Anaheim, captured *here and overleaf* with all the favourite Disney characters, from "Mickey Mouse" to "Tigger", delights children and adults alike. Two of the most popular methods of transport in this fantastic wonderland are by monorail *above right* and by the delightful Mark Twain Riverboat *bottom right* which cruises down the river passing Tom Sawyer's Island and Fort Wilderness.

The fabulous J. Paul Getty Museum *right* was built in the style of a 1st century Roman villa to house a superb collection of antiquities, paintings and furnishings and was opened to the public in January 1974.

Joshua Tree National Monument *pictured on this page* lies between two vast deserts, the low Colorado and the high Mojave. It receives its name from the Joshua tree, a giant member of the lily family and the most famous of all the species contained in this incredible desert.

Mission San Gabriel Archangel with its beautiful cloisters *right* was the fourth mission to be dedicated in California. Of a striking and unusual design, the church incorporates many Moorish features and is maintained by the traditionalist Claretian Fathers. Now one of the most splendid sights in California, Mission Inn *far right* was started in 1875 as an adobe cottage. This magnificent mission houses many treasures including the St Francis Chapel and the Garden of the Bells.

Palm Springs, an international playground for the wealthy, stands in desert bordered on the west by the San Jacinto Mountains and the fabulous aerial views *above, centre right and left* show the beautifully manicured Walter Annenberg Estate.

Of all sporting activities within the Palm Springs area golf is supreme. This "Golf Capital of the World" contains many courses, all of which remain green throughout the year and the Del Safari Country Club *top right and far left* is just one superb example. Polo is also popular within the community and *right* can be seen a vigorous game at the El Dorado Polo Club, Indian Wells, played against the magnificent mountain backdrop.

Swinging high between the mountains of San Jacinto is the Palm Springs tramway *above and near left,* justly described as "the eighth engineering masterpiece of the world". Perched, incredibly, on a mountain plateau in this isolated terrain, lies Bob Hope's house *far left,* and *right,* looking like a giant checker-board is Palm Springs seen from the air. In the "Living Desert Reserve" near Palm Springs *top and centre right* are still more of the remarkable cacti and desert blooms, so prolific in springtime. The beautiful meadowland in the Palomar Mountain District is shown *overleaf.*

The old missions of Southern California are part of its rich heritage and many are centrally placed within the city that grew around them. On the Carmel-Monterey Peninsula is the lovely Mission of San Carlos Borromeo de Carmelo *left* and *below* stands the whitewashed Mission at Santa Barbara with its picturesque pink relief.

San Juan Bautista whose Mission *left and centre left* was founded in 1797, is the largest church in California and *below* is the pretty old mission of San Luis Rey de Francis.

With elegant tiled fountains gracing its gardens is Mission San Buenaventura *above and top right*, the last to be founded by Father Serra.

The delightful courtyard of Mission Juan Capistrano can be seen *right*, the church having been founded in 1776, American Independence Year, and *below* in this tranquil setting stands the Mission of San Luis Obispo. Another fine view *bottom right* of San Carlos Borremeo de Carmelo.

Beautiful Santa Barbara *above* has a magnificent Court House *left and far left* set in lovely landscaped gardens, whilst *right* is the exquisite church-like Assembly Room and Meeting Place contained within its interior. El Paseo *below* with its picturesque al fresco cáfes is built in and around historic adobes and *above right* can be seen the windmill and quaint thatched houses in the Danish Community of Solvang.

Perched atop San Simeon's "Enchanted Hill" stands the Hearst Castle, dominated by the central building of La Casa Grande. There are, within the estate, terraced gardens with marble statues, pools and guest houses *this page* and a collection of wildlife. Many treasures and buildings were imported from Europe, such as the Greek Temple *above,* which was re-assembled along the edge of the fantastic romanesque pool.

The 576 foot Morro Rock guards the entrance to the Bay *left,* and *overleaf left* can be seen the Bixby Creek Bridge on Highway 1 in rugged Monterey County and *right* sunset falls on the crashing waves along the Big Sur coast.

The wild rugged coastline, so much a feature of Big Sur in Monterey, is seen here in differing moods; crashing waves pound the rocks *top left* whilst *above and centre left* the calmer Pacific Ocean laps the coves.

A challenge to all golfers is the 7th hole at Pebble Beach Golf Links *bottom left*.

The pretty Victorian house in Salinas *below* was once the childhood home of novelist John Steinbeck.

Memorable Monterey with historic
Cannery Row *above and bottom right*,
the original of which was immortalised
by Steinbeck, has many reminders of
the past. Now a museum, the pretty,
Pacific House with its veranda *top right*
stands in the State Park and *below,* in
sharp contrast of styles, is the ultra-
modern Doubletree Inn and Convention
Centre. The tightly packed harbour,
sited on the crescent bay, can be seen
below.

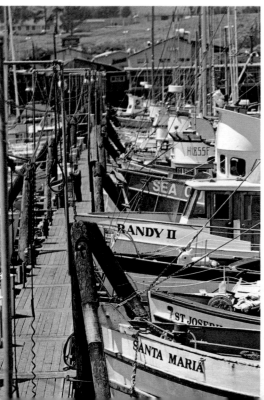

Napa Valley is wine country in California and it contains many excellent wineries, among them the Sterling Vineyards at Calistoga *above left and centre left* and the Beringer Winery at St Helena *above*: in the Salinas Valley near Greenfield is the Wente Brothers Arroyo Seco Vineyards *bottom left.* "Old Faithful" near Calistoga *below* is an incredible geyser which spurts a 60 foot jet of vapour and steam every 50 minutes.

California St *right,* looking out over the Oakland Bay Bridge, parodies San Francisco's love for development and tradition alike.

San Francisco and Oakland are pictured in the background *above* as the Golden Gate Bridge spans the bay.

Although a poor imitation of the original Barbary Coast which emerged in the days of the 'Gold Rush' in California, Broadway, San Francisco, with its blazing lights, bars, clubs and restaurants *left*, still attracts many visitors.

One of the most picturesque streets in San Francisco is Lombard *right* which winds tortuously downhill between Leavenworth and Hyde, affording magnificent views to drivers and pedestrians alike. By contrast the almost vertical Fresnol St *above right* rises precipitously and on the brow can be seen one of the city's famous cable cars.

As night falls over San Francisco's Oakland Bay Bridge *overleaf* the calm waters reflect the glow from the glittering lights along the shoreline.

Bridgeport *centre left* in Mono County is set in a luxuriant valley *top left* and was once called "Big Meadow". Within the county can be seen Sonora Pass *below right*; and *bottom left* more magnificent mountain scenery whose beauty is matched by the blue waters of Mono Lake *below*.

One of the most spectacular of all National Parks, Yosemite, whose fantastic falls can be seen *above right*, also contains within its precipitous mountains the sheer delicate falls of Bridalveil *overleaf* and *above* with Merced River in the foreground.

Once the rowdiest gold mining town in the West and now a mouldering spectre town, Bodie *this page* has been maintained as a State Historic Park. At the peak of its notoriety it boasted over 65 saloons and a murder a day was purportedly committed. The fast flowing icy rivers of Dana *overleaf left* and Merced *overleaf right* are set in the beautiful Yosemite National Park.

On the south-western shore of Lake Tahoe lies Emerald Bay with the splendid Eagle Falls *above* cascading past the massed pines into the lake beyond. Set like a jewel in the bay's blue waters is Emerald Island *top right*.

Threading its way along the floor of the Yosemite Valley is the Merced River seen *left* with the towering Cathedral Spires in the background. Numerous falls and lakes feature in California's various parks and valleys and two beautiful examples can be seen in the Cascade Falls *right* and Tenaya Lake *far left*.

Collected together *on this page* is a variety of pictures showing the diversity of California's scenery: the saloon at Mokelumne Hill *above,* Silver Lake *top left,* Calaveras Big Trees in the State Park *left,* and Indian Grinding Rock *bottom left,* pictured next to which is a cab of Placerville's Fire Dept. The building *below* is in Columbia Historic Park and *right* is shown the end of the road at the Sacramento County Line. *Overleaf* is pictured one of San Francisco's famous street musicians.

First published in Great Britain 1978 by Colour Library International Ltd.
© Illustrations: Colour Library International Ltd. Colour separations by La Cromolito, Milan, Italy.
Display and text filmsetting by Focus Photoset, London, England.
Printed and bound by Group Poligrafici Calderara - Bologna - Italy
Published by Crescent Books, a division of Crown Publishers Inc.
Library of Congress Catalogue Card No. 78-59737
CRESCENT 1978